Seven Letters to Seven Churches
Breaking the Bread of Revelation
Volume 2

Seven Letters to Seven Churches
Breaking the Bread of Revelation
Volume 2

Brian McCallum

Brian McCallum Ministries
4202 W. Toledo Court
Broken Arrow, OK 74012

Seven Letters to Seven Churches,
Breaking the Bread of Revelation, Volume 2
Published by:
Brian McCallum Ministries
12645 E. 127th St.
Broken Arrow, OK 74011
ISBN 0-9620883-1-5

Sixth Printing, July 2003

Editorial Consultant: Phyllis Mackall, Broken Arrow, Oklahoma

Cover design and book production by:
Double Blessing Productions
16 1/2 N. Park St. Sapulpa, OK 74066
www.doubleblessing.com
Cover illustration is protected by the 1976 United States Copyright Act.
Copyright © 1989 by Double Blessing Productions

Printed in the United States of America.

Dedication

To my wife, June, with ever-increasing love and admiration.

You are an inspiration to me as you walk in the love of Jesus.

One reason why I know His life-changing power is because I see Him in you.

Contents

Preface

The second and third chapters of Revelation consist of seven letters (or epistles) addressed to seven churches.

In these letters, we see the Head of the Church, the Lord Jesus Christ, ministering to the whole Church, His Body, for the whole Age of Grace.

These letters summarize His commendations for, warnings to, and promises to overcomers — believers who are living in Christ, growing in Christ, obeying His commandments.

All of these letters are entirely consistent with other New Testament writings, and they are as applicable to us today as they were when the Apostle John wrote them under the unction of the Holy Spirit and sent them to the seven churches in Asia.

These seven short epistles continue the emphasis on the Church of Jesus Christ and its mission in this world: to proclaim the good news of our Redemption and our Redeemer, the Lord Jesus Christ.

These seven letters point the way to what is found in the subsequent four chapters of Revelation — the victorious conclusion to the Age of Grace.

Listen with your heart as the Head of the Church ministers to His Body!

Seven Letters to Seven Churches
Breaking the Bread of Revelation
Volume 2

Chapter 1
The Church in Ephesus

Unto the angel of the church of Ephesus write; These things saith he that holdeth the seven stars in his right hand, who walketh in the midst of the seven golden candlesticks.

I know thy works, and thy labour, and thy patience, and how thou canst not bear them which are evil: and thou hast tried them which say they are apostles, and are not, and hast found them liars.

And hast borne, and hast patience, and for my name's sake hast laboured, and hast not fainted.

Nevertheless, I have somewhat against thee, because thou hast left thy first love.

Remember therefore from whence thou art fallen, and repent, and do the first works; or else I will come unto thee quickly, and will remove thy candlestick out of his place, except thou repent.

But this thou hast, that thou hatest the deeds of the Nicolaitanes, which I also hate.

He that hath an ear, let him hear what the Spirit saith unto the churches; To him that overcometh will I give to eat of the tree of life, which is in the midst of the paradise of God.

Revelation 2:1-7

Historical and Geographical Background

The letter to Ephesus has special significance, because it is the first of the letters addressed to the seven churches in Asia.

Ephesus was the largest and most important city in first century A.D. Asia. This "Asia," a Roman province, comprised the westernmost third of the modern nation of Turkey. All of the seven churches of Revelation 2 and 3 were located in this province.

These churches were founded under the ministry of the Apostle Paul; they were begun during his second missionary journey, in approximately A.D. 55. Some of the church history of that period is related in the following verses from Acts 19:

> **And it came to pass, that, while Apollos was at Corinth, Paul having passed through the upper coasts came to Ephesus: and finding certain disciples,**
>
> **He said unto them, Have ye received the Holy Ghost since ye believed? And they said unto him, We have not so much as heard whether there be any Holy Ghost.**
>
> **And he said unto them, Unto what then were ye baptized? And they said, Unto John's baptism.**
>
> **Then said Paul, John verily baptized with the baptism of repentance, saying unto the people, that they should believe on him which should come after him, that is, on Christ Jesus.**
>
> **When they heard this, they were baptized in the name of the Lord Jesus.**
>
> **And when Paul had laid his hands upon them, the Holy Ghost came on them; and they spake with tongues, and prophesied.**
>
> **And all the men were about twelve.**

> And he went into the synagogue, and spake boldly for the space of three months, disputing and persuading the things concerning the kingdom of God.
>
> But when divers were hardened, and believed not, but spake evil of that way before the multitude, he departed from them, and separated the disciples, disputing daily in the school of one Tyrannus.
>
> And this continued by the space of two years; so that all they which dwelt in Asia heard the word of the Lord Jesus, both Jews and Greeks....
>
> So he [Paul] sent into Macedonia two of them that ministered unto him, Timotheus and Erastus; but he himself stayed in Asia for a season....
>
> Moreover ye see and hear, that not alone at Ephesus, but almost throughout all Asia, this Paul hath persuaded and turned away much people, saying that they be no gods, which are made with hands.
>
> Acts 19:1-10,22,26

Ephesus, by John's time, was the Roman capital of Asia, chosen because of its location as a major seaport at the convergence of the major roads and trade routes from Europe to Asia.

Except for those already converted to Christ, it was populated by lusty, sensual people who had prospered greatly in the natural sense, but were devoutly pagan.

The temple of the goddess Diana (Artemis), one of the seven wonders of the ancient world, was located in Ephesus, and attracted many visitors.

This pagan temple with its idol goddess was a great satanic influence locally and the cause of much adversity in the Apostle Paul's life and, I am sure, in the lives of all the faithful in that region.

For instance, the worship of the Roman emperor as a god was very strong in Ephesus, due in large part to the satanic stronghold surrounding worship of the goddess Diana.

Eusebius and Irenaeus, early fathers and historians of the first and second century Church, both relate that Ephesus became the home of the Apostle John. John was said to have brought Mary, the mother of Jesus, there to live out her days on earth under his care and protection. John was the leader of the Ephesian church prior to his exile to Patmos, where he received the Revelation.

The letters to the seven churches were received by John some 35 to 40 years after the founding of those churches. The beginning of the seven letters is found in Revelation 2:1, which reads, "Unto the angel of the church of Ephesus write; These things saith he that holdeth the seven stars in his right hand...."

Who is seated at the right hand of God? Jesus! And He says He's holding the seven stars in His right hand. That means, all who are saved are there, seated with Him in heavenly places.

The Candlesticks Reflect Jesus Christ

Revelation 2:1 continues, "...who walketh in the midst of the seven golden candlesticks." Jesus walks in the midst of the Church, doesn't He? Thus, Jesus is represented to this world by the seven churches — no *other* way.

And whatever God does in the earth — no matter how supernatural it may be, no matter how wonderful, no matter what a great sign or wonder it is — it does not happen because Jesus came to do it independently of the Church. Jesus came to do these things *through* the Church. He is represented to this world and to everyone in it by these seven churches. They are the

4

candlesticks. They are the *light* of the world, as Jesus said in Matthew 5.

Revelation 2:1 continues, "I know thy works, and thy labour. . . ." You'll notice that Jesus commends the Ephesians for different things, but not a great deal is said about their works. When Jesus does commend them for works, are they works of the flesh? Are they things you would do, depending on your natural ability (or the energy of the flesh)? No.

Works Produced by Faith

You'll always do a lot of natural work in the ministry of the Gospel, but what Jesus is commending the Ephesians for is their works that proceed from faith. Real faith produces works, doesn't it? Faith without works is — what? Dead — being alone. So faith without works is really not faith; it's dead. Faith is a living thing.

So Jesus is commending the Ephesians for works that proceed from faith, hope and love — works that will abide forever. He says, "I know thy works, and thy labour, and thy patience [patience is a fruit of the spirit], and how thou canst not bear them which are evil: and thou hast tried them which say they are apostles, and are not, and hast found them liars" (v. 2).

There are people going around even today proclaiming themselves to be lots of things. They claim they are apostles, prophets, pastors, teachers, or evangelists — and they aren't any of these things! God didn't appoint them to those offices. They are trying to appoint themselves.

In the first century, there was a great deal of that going on. Paul warned about it over and over again in the epistles. He warned the churches not to accept ministry from men who advanced themselves; men who proclaimed themselves to be something. He said in Second Corinthians 11:14,15, "And no marvel; for Satan himself is transformed into an angel of light. Therefore it is no great thing if his ministers also be transformed as the ministers of righteousness. . . ."

Paul is saying, "They appear to be like apostles, but the devil appears to be an angel of light, and he's the one who's sending them."

Judging the Supernatural

Just because something is supernatural doesn't mean it's from God! This is why we judge all things by God's Word. God has given us revelation in the Word so we can do it. If we want to stay in the middle of the road, we must understand what His Word says. Otherwise, we're eligible to be deluded, misled, and dragged off to one side or the other.

Now Jesus says, "They're not apostles, and you have found them to be liars. And hast borne, and hast patience, and for my name's sake hast laboured, and hast not fainted" (v. 3).

When the Bible speaks of fainting, especially in the New Testament, what is it referring to? Giving up. Backing away. Withdrawing. Sometimes when people face difficulties, or they run into fierce opposition, they think, "Well, I must be out of God's will."

To tell you the truth, the more opposition you're finding to your ministry, the more it proves that you *are* in God's will and you have a powerful ministry! If you didn't, the devil wouldn't be wasting his time trying to stop you. *Opposition is not a bad thing.* Opposition is not something that we ought to run away from, ever.

Direction by Circumstances

God will not deal with you by negative circumstances to guide you. That's a flat statement. God will guide you in your spirit. He'll tell you when to come and when to go and what to do. But He won't leave it up to circumstances that are going on around you to tell you what to do.

Some people have gone out after hearing from God. He said to go to such and such a place and labor in that vineyard. So they went and labored, and nothing happened for a year. In fact, everything looked *worse* than when they arrived!

Is that a reason they ought to go somewhere else? That's *never* a reason you ought to go somewhere else. Until God tells you to go somewhere else, stay where He sent you.

Now I know we're not always a hundred percent accurate in hearing the voice of God — none of us is. But if you seek Him, what will happen? You'll *find* Him. So keep seeking until you're satisfied that you have found God and heard from Him. Seek *Him*, however; don't seek what happens around you as His direction to you.

God can speak to you individually, can't He? He has that ability, and you've developed the capacity to commune with Him. Use it and depend on it. The more you do, the more He'll be able to speak to you through it. So don't faint.

Rebuke and Reproof

Everything Jesus has said up to this point has been good. Jesus has commended the church of Ephesus for all their good works. But now He's going to to rebuke and reprove the Ephesians. He's going to bring up some things that need to be corrected.

He begins the fourth verse, "Nevertheless, I have somewhat against thee, because thou hast left thy first love. Remember therefore from whence thou art fallen, and repent, and do the first works; or else I will come unto thee quickly, and will remove thy candlestick out of his place, except thou repent."

Notice that whenever Jesus warns them about anything in these epistles, He always says, "Repent." That's the correction for their error. That's always the correction for a believer when he hears the truth. When a believer realizes he has been in sin or he has been doing something wrong, the correction is always to repent.

What does the word "repent" mean? Turn around. Do it differently. You are free to do that. God has made you free. He set you free from all the authorities, principalities, and powers that could bind you. All of the fleshly influences. All of the worldly influences. You are free from all of them in Christ. Therefore, you can turn around, make a decision, and do things differently in the power of God in your life. You're free to do it.

When we see that, we ought to repent, for we really do not have any reason not to. God expects us to walk in the light we have. When we have received light by hearing the Word of God, we have no reason not to obey it. We can obey it. We are free to obey it. There is revelation. Through or by the help of the Holy Ghost, you receive illumination. And when you have that, Jesus says to walk in that light.

Now Jesus says in this fifth verse, "repent, and do the first works. . ." He said you left your first love. Go back and do the first works over again, "or else I will come unto thee quickly, and will remove thy candlestick out of his place, except thou repent."

The Fruit of Unrepentance

Jesus is *not* telling this church that the *immediate* result of anything they have done wrong or are doing wrong is that they're going to be cast out of the kingdom of heaven. That's not what this passage means.

What Jesus does mean is that *eventually*, somewhere down the line, there will be repercussions from their acts. Maybe it won't happen in their own generation, but there will come a time when the church will no longer be alive unto God. Why? Because if you tolerate things that bring death, eventually death will come!

I know this is true from personal experience. I was raised in a church like that. It was deader than the proverbial doorknob. It didn't have any Gospel in it. Oh, we knew that God existed, and we knew that Jesus Christ was His Son, but we didn't have the foggiest idea that we were supposed to have a personal relationship with Him. No one ever said so.

Yet, at one time, that was a live denomination — as live as could be. And it is again today. It's being revived. The very congregation I was raised in has gone through a period of revival during the last six years, and the people are beginning to get saved. Thank God! But it was a long time to wait.

I remember one preacher who came was really sent by God to preach the Gospel. He didn't last very long. I think he preached the Word a few Sundays, and they ran him out!

That's what happens when you've got a church that controls its destiny by the vote. When they're backslidden, they don't vote for revival; they vote for the status quo! They want to keep that self-satisfied, dumb, dead feeling. It takes a real move of the Holy Ghost to break up that kind of fallow ground.

So Jesus is warning this church at Ephesus, which is alive, which He has commended, that if they don't reverse their trend toward coolness, this is where they will end up. He tells them to repent. In other words, He's saying the ball is in their court; now it's up to them to do something.

Once God has shown you what's wrong, it's up to you to do something about it. You aren't supposed to get down on your knees and say, "O God, now do it for me." God has already done something for you: He has given you His Word. Now you need to be obedient to it. As you see the light in the Word, obey it. You don't need to receive a *special* revelation; you need the revelation that you saw in the Word of God.

Don't be like the man who heard a sermon on the importance of tithing and got up and said, "I want everyone to pray for me that I'll tithe." At that point, you have no need for any more prayer. Just do what the Word says!

How Preachers Lose Their First Love

"Remember therefore from whence thou art fallen, and repent, and do the first works. . . ." Jesus is saying that if you leave your first love, you need to go back and do the first works over again.

What is He referring to? What had the Ephesians fallen away from? There is an easy trap ministers and others fall into: As they get into the ministry, they find out how much work is involved, and they get very busy — too busy for God! That's the way it usually happens. You get used to working for God, and you are working for God, believe me. You are working *hard!* When I retired from the Air Force and went into the ministry, I never worked harder in my life.

The thing that happens in the beginning of our relationship is that we are totally dependent on God. Totally! Think about the day you got saved: How much did you depend on yourself at that point, and how much did you depend on God? The greatest miracle you ever experienced happened in your life because you depended on Him, didn't it?

Now Jesus says, "Don't return to depending on what you can do — depending on yourself and depending on your works." Yes, the works should be there — Jesus commends the Ephesians for having the works — but we're not to *depend* on the works. We're not to *trust* in the works.

Trust in God

We are to trust in God and only in Him. And the more we grow in the knowledge of God, the more we ought to trust in Him; not in anything we've learned, which is still in part only. We do learn things, don't we? For instance, we learn how to flow with the Holy Ghost.

Are you going to trust one experience, or are you going to trust Jesus? What if He doesn't move the same way every time? (And He won't.) You can't put God in a box. You've got to learn to trust in Him even more as you grow in your Christian life than you did in the beginning!

The tendency of human beings, because we live our natural way so much of the time, is to resume trusting in what we knew how to do before we were saved. So Jesus says to go back to that place where we began to trust and once again depend totally on Him and look to Him for everything.

Just because you got wonderfully anointed last Sunday doesn't mean you can *presume* to have that same anointing from now on. No, you will need to do what you did in spiritual preparation, plus more, to have that anointing again.

Learn to continually trust in Jesus, keeping that trust fresh and new in your relationship, just like it was in the beginning, when you depended totally upon Him, and you were looking to Him for everything.

After all, Jesus is the Head of the Body. We may be in a position of authority over a few people, but that doesn't make us the Head. Jesus is the Head. We are undershepherds. We minister to people in local groups, or congregations.

We will be promoted into positions of authority when we become competent in certain areas, but the fact that we gain some competency in an area doesn't mean we should be less dependent on the Head of the Church. We should always strive to become more dependent on the Head of the Church!

So don't leave that place of your first love. Keep it fresh. Keep it stirred up in you. Keep your dependence on the Lord. Let Him know how much you depend on Him daily.

I have found that confessing the truth causes it to come to pass. I confess my dependence on Jesus over and over again. By doing this, I find that I work and move in that dependency more than if I had taken it for granted. We shouldn't take our dependency on the Lord for granted.

Jesus said He would remove the Ephesians' candlestick if they didn't repent from trusting in their own works. Doing so would eventually bring death to their church, as we saw earlier.

Jesus Tells Us What He Hates

In verse 6, Jesus resumes commending the Ephesians: "But this thou hast, that thou hatest the deeds of the Nicolaitanes, which I also hate."

The word "Nicolaitanes" is a combination of two Greek words — one meaning "victorious over" and the other meaning "ordinary people." I think the Nicolaitanes invented these words "clergy" and "laity"; God didn't. God didn't say, "These are the clergy and these are the laity, and the former shall be above the latter."

I don't think God even likes those words. Why? Because every believer is a member of one Body. Everyone is "a member in particular." Clergymen are members in particular because they have a calling on their life, and they're in a position that God put them in. They're essential in the Body for His purposes. That gift should be respected and submitted to, but that doesn't mean that the rest of the members of the Body aren't essential.

In fact, the Word teaches just the opposite. It says some of the members of the Body that you don't see very often are the most important ones, or worthy of the most honor! It likens this to your own body. (See First Corinthians 12:18-25.)

Think about the hidden parts of your body. Take your liver, for example. Whoever sees your liver? You wouldn't want to! But how long could you live without it? How about your lungs? They're not beautiful to look at, and they're not something that people look at very often, are they? But how long could you live without them?

All the parts of the human body are necessary. Every part, even if it's a little toe, helps you. If you lost a toe, you would need to learn how to walk in a new way, because you would lose a great deal of the natural balance you used to have.

All Members Are Equal

The comparison that Jesus makes to the human body is excellent. I'm so glad that our wonderfully made flesh can be used as an example, because the human body teaches us many things about the Body of Christ. It teaches about the interdependence in the Body of Christ and about how all the members of the Body are equally important.

What these Nicolaitanes were doing was saying that there was a group in the Body that was more important than anyone else, so everyone had to look up to them. This error was part of Gnosticism. Their thinking was, "You must depend on these people, or you won't get to know God." This philosophy put men in the place that God alone should have. That's why Jesus hated their deeds.

The Gnostics also taught men that God is holy and that all material things, including man's natural body, are unholy. Therefore, they reasoned, "It doesn't make any difference what you do in the natural. Do whatever you want in the flesh — if it feels good, do it." (That's a modern Gnostic statement.)

You can see how wrong that philosophy is. The Word of God says that you have been bought with a price. What was the price? Jesus Christ and His blood. That is the highest price that could ever have been paid. *And it was paid!* Therefore, glorify God in your body and in your spirit, which are God's, the Bible says (1 Corinthians 6:19,20).

Jesus purchased your *body*, didn't He? He didn't just purchase your *spirit*. He purchased you — your whole being. Therefore, we are to glorify God in our whole man. And we are not to take a careless attitude toward natural or spiritual living.

Again, the Nicolaitanes were doing just that. They were dividing the Body of Christ into clergy and laity. They were also teaching such false doctrines as it doesn't matter what you do in the natural. In fact, it does matter. It makes a great deal of difference! That's why Jesus hated their deeds.

The Tree of Life

Jesus resumes His message to the churches in verse 7: "He that hath an ear, let him hear what the Spirit saith unto the churches; To him that overcometh will I give to eat of the tree of life, which is in the midst of the paradise of God."

The tree of life is mentioned in the third chapter of Genesis; it was in the midst of the Garden of Eden. Verse 22 says that God drove Adam and Eve out of the garden, ". . . lest he put forth his hand, and take also of the tree of life, and eat, and live for ever."

Why did God not want them to partake of the tree of life once they had fallen and become separated from Him? Because they would have lived *forever* separated from God! As it was, they lived more than nine hundred years afterwards.

How would you like to live nine hundred years without ever being born again? I don't think I would like that. (It was bad enough living thirty-two years without being born again.)

Because God drove Adam and Eve out of the garden, we have the idea that this was a type of punishment, but it wasn't a punishment at all. It was the best thing that God could do for them at that point!

God Had a Plan

After driving them out of the garden, He stationed "at the east of the garden of Eden Cherubims, and a flaming sword which turneth every way, to keep the way of the tree of life" (v. 24). God had a purpose in all of this. We always assumed this was simply to prevent them from getting back into the Garden of Eden.

I can remember a big mural that decorated our Sunday School room when I was a little boy. It showed a big, old man. He had a lot of white hair and He was holding something in His hand. (This was supposed to be God.) He was very angry.

Adam and Eve were depicted slinking out of the garden with an expression that seemed to say, "Don't hit me again, God!" The mural also showed the serpent and a half-eaten apple laying on the ground. (I don't know why they thought it was an apple, but they did.)

That's not the way it was! When God drove Adam and Eve away from the garden, it was for their own good. Furthermore, there is symbolism in the cherubim He stationed with the flaming sword that turned every way.

A cherub is a supernatural being, symbolizing or representing the Spirit of God, and that flaming sword symbolizes the Word of God!

The cherubim were "to keep the way of the tree of life." Jesus said, "I am the *way,* the truth, and the life." God was preserving the way in the earth, wasn't He? He was preserving His way. Not man's way; His way. God preserved the spiritual way of faith in the earth by excluding them naturally from the garden.

A Promise for Overcomers

In Revelation 2:7, we saw where Jesus said, "To him that overcometh will I give to eat of the tree of life. . . ." How do you *overcome?* By what? By the blood of the Lamb (Revelation 12:11). You overcome by His blood and by your agreement with the Word of God [the word of your testimony]. Therefore, you do what? You partake of that tree as an overcomer!

Proverbs 15:4 gives us a good look at what an overcomer does. It says, "A wholesome tongue is a tree of life. . . ." A wholesome tongue is one who is speaking the Word of God. It's one who speaks from a believing heart. The verse concludes, "but perverseness therein is a breach in the spirit." That describes one who speaks only from sense knowledge and amplifies the problem. But a wholesome tongue is *a tree of life!*

So the cherubim and the flaming sword were placed east of the garden to preserve the way of eternal life. Jesus said, "I am the way, the truth and the life" (John 14:6). Has that way been kept? Yes.

The tree of life's placement in the Garden of Eden was one of the first moves God made to show Adam and Eve how to return to that eternal life they had departed from.

God warned them, "But of the tree of the knowledge of good and evil, thou shalt not eat of it: for in the day that thou eatest thereof thou shalt surely die" (Genesis 2:17). *They died spiritually the day they disobeyed,* and eventually they also died *naturally.*

Yet during the remainder of their human life on earth, they had the opportunity to understand what had happened and return to trusting in God.

We can see from the testimony of Genesis that Adam and Eve *did* return to God! The Bible says that in Seth's day, men began to call upon the name of the Lord. Adam was still alive then. What happens when you call upon the Name of the Lord? You're saved!

The Name they called on is the same Name you called on: the Savior, Jesus Christ. God showed them that He would come. He showed this to them there in the garden, right after they sinned (Genesis 3:15,20,21). They began to realize that it was true, and they began to call on that Name.

God saw their faith, and He counted it to them for right-standing, didn't He? So God kept the way of the tree of life.

Rewards Are Not Postponed

In Revelation 2:7, we also saw that Jesus said, "To him that overcometh will I give to eat...." I want you to see something about overcomers. Jesus is not saying that *someday in the future,* you'll get to be on top of everything — *if* you grit your teeth and bear it during this lifetime. He's not saying that at all.

He's telling those who learn how to live in their God-given privileges *now,* "You will have the fulfillment and completion of all of this at the end." But He is not postponing the overcomers' reward until then. It's yours now, too, isn't it, as you believe the Word of God?

You'll not be overcomers only in that great day when you'll be gathered together to be with the Lord. You're overcomers now! Now is the time to overcome.

There won't be anything to *overcome* in the hereafter, when you're out of this world; when the Lord has come and gathered you to Himself and you have gone to be with Him in heaven. There will be nothing there to overcome! There's no world system in heaven. No flesh. No devil. Those are the only things you've got to overcome now, so now is the time to overcome, isn't it?

Schools in Heaven?

That's one reservation I have concerning teaching that there are schools in heaven. Such teachings can lead people to believe, "Well, if I don't learn it here and now, I will catch up when I get up there."

I am sure that we will *always* be learning more about an infinite God. However, there are certain things that our God has ordained for us to learn in *this* lifetime. They relate directly to the course or race set before us now (Second Timothy 4:6-8).

I have searched my Bible, and I can find no reference to our being schooled in the hereafter. If we are, there will be one element of learning missing: the opportunity to apply what we have learned through experiencing tests or trials, like we do now in this present life.

How will you overcome in heaven, where there's nothing to overcome, and there never will be? When Jesus returns, and you reign on the earth with Him, there won't be anything for you, a glorified saint, to overcome here, either. That's why it's important for you to understand that we overcome now, in this lifetime.

Finish *your* race. Finish *your* course with joy. It's set before you so you will be fully qualified and fully developed in every area of the spiritual man.

An overcomer is someone who lives and moves and has his being in Christ. An overcomer learns how to do that to the highest degree. Paul said at one point in his life, "You know my life is just about over. I have finished my race." Would you like to finish yours? Keep running. You already know who wins: *You win!* Just finish the race.

It's not like you're running to see whether you win or not. You already know you win. We *all* win this race; there is no competition between saints. Just finish it, and you will have everything God wants you to have; you will be everything God made you to be, for all eternity.

Chapter 2
The Church in Smyrna

And unto the angel of the church in Smyrna write;
These things saith the first and the last, which was
dead, and is alive.

I know thy works, and tribulation, and poverty,
(but thou art rich) and I know the blasphemy of them
which say they are Jews, and are not, but are the
synagogue of Satan.

Fear none of those things which thou shalt suffer:
behold, the devil shall cast some of you into prison
that ye may be tried; and ye shall have tribulation ten
days: be thou faithful unto death, and I will give thee
a crown of life.

He that hath an ear, let him hear what the Spirit
saith unto the churches; He that overcometh shall not
be hurt of the second death.

Revelation 2:8-11

Historical and Geographical Background

Smyrna was called the loveliest city in Asia. It was
located on the Mediterranean seacoast, surrounded
by coastal hills and low mountains.

The city, an old Greek colony, had been most
recently rebuilt by Lysimachus, one of Alexander the
Great's generals. It had long, wide streets, stately
buildings, and a continual sea breeze that refreshed the
city in all seasons.

Smyrna had early on become loyal to Rome and was later an enthusiastic participant in the renewed emperor worship that swept through the Roman Empire in the early and mid-second century.

This was one city where the Early Church endured increasing tribulation and persecution which reached its zenith with the martyrdom of Polycarp, a disciple of the Apostle John and the Bishop of Smyrna at the time of his death.

Polycarp was publicly burned at the stake because he refused to worship the Roman emperor and renounce his Lord and Savior, Jesus Christ. His answer to the Roman proconsul echoes down through the centuries: "Eighty and six years have I served Him, and He never did me wrong; and how can I now blaspheme my King that has saved me?"

Smyrna, in the day of the Apostle John's letter, had a population of 200,000, and was a busy seaport and center of trade. The modern city of Izmir, Turkey, with a population of more than two million, stands on the site of ancient Smyrna.

Tribulation and Poverty

Jesus addresses the church in Smyrna by referring to Himself as "the first and the last." Who is that? Jesus of Nazareth! He's the First and the Last, the Alpha and the Omega, the Beginning and the Ending.

He as God has no beginning. He as God has no ending. He as man is the beginning and the fulfillment of the Church. He is the Author and the Finisher of our faith. He is the Word of God, which shall never pass away.

In verse 9, Jesus says, "I know thy works, and tribulation, and poverty, (but thou art rich) and I know the blasphemy of them which say they are Jews, and are not, but are the synagogue of Satan."

Again, Jesus is referring to the good works done by the Christians in Smyrna — works that proceed from faith, hope, and love.

Jesus also mentions their "tribulation and poverty." In other words, Jesus is commending this church for their faithfulness in the midst of trials — trials like those the Apostle Paul said he had experienced many times.

Jesus is not commending them for being poverty-stricken, however. That's not the will of God. He says, "...but thou art *rich*." Why can He call them rich? Because they were laying up a different kind of treasure: spiritual treasure in heaven.

If you lay up spiritual treasure in heaven, you can say, with Paul, that you have learned to be content, no matter what state you're in, because you know God is your Provider. You can say, "I know God can meet my need, and I know He always does, whether that need be of my spirit, soul, or body."

Laying Aside Privileges

Sometimes to be effective in the ministry, you must lay aside some of your privileges and rights to the natural prosperity we are promised in the Gospel, which varies widely from culture to culture. For example, what if the Lord told you, "Go up the Amazon River, turn left on the third tributary, and go about ten miles and work for Me there?"

You're not going to be able to take your Cadillac, your nice ranch house, or your checkbook with you on that canoe. What would you do with checks in the middle of a jungle, anyway?

No, you've got to lay aside some of your privileges and natural blessings to obey God's call and to serve Him under those conditions. And that's not bad; that's good. That's what Jesus means. He is saying you won't be sorry you served Him sacrificially. You will rejoice one day over the treasure you have laid up in heaven.

God doesn't deprive you of things. Whenever God says, "Lay something down," He always gives you something *better* in its place. When you paddle up that tributary in obedience to God's call, find out what God sent you to do there, and do it, you'll rejoice all the more.

So don't get to the point in your life where you're so bound by material things, position, or personal preference that you're not free to answer God's call.

In the last part of verse 9, Jesus discusses those who "say they are Jews, and are not, but are the synagogue of Satan." He's talking about Jews from the church back in Jerusalem who went around trying to teach believers in every place that Paul and the apostles had preached, to return to Jewish legalism (or works).

Professed Christians

Jesus calls them "the synagogue of Satan." And He says they blaspheme. These people who said they were Jews (and weren't) put us in mind of the majority of professed Christians of our age.

There are many today who say they are Christians and are not. I know how this is, because for many years I was one of them! Evangelical and Word-oriented Christians are often opposed and put down today by such people who say they are Christians but are not.

When such people criticize the true Church, they are blaspheming. They are speaking in the spirit of anti-Christ. They are really speaking against God! Their speaking can and will translate into harassing and persecuting actions against the Church — much as Paul himself was doing against the Early Church until the Lord arrested him.

Jesus continues in verse 10, "Fear none of those things which thou shalt suffer: behold, the devil shall cast some of you into prison, that ye may be tried; and ye shall have tribulation ten days: be thou faithful unto death, and I will give thee a crown of life."

This Is the Will of God?

These believers in Smyrna must really be out of the will of God, right? They must have missed it somewhere for something this drastic to happen to them. What a disgrace!

But Paul and Silas didn't consider it a disgrace to be in prison. What did they do at midnight when they were locked in the stocks with their backs bleeding? They rejoiced, didn't they? And God came and delivered them out of their plight.

So it was not a disgrace for them to be clapped into a prison. It would have been if they'd been stealing from the citizens of Philippi, but they weren't. Paul and Silas weren't in prison because of wrongdoing; they were there because they did right! For this, they got beaten raw, clamped into stocks, and thrown into prison.

It would have been very easy for them to have said, "Well, we must have missed God somewhere," wouldn't it? Too often we look at our circumstances and think that these *circumstances* are an indicator of whether or not God is pleased with what we're doing.

However, if we look to circumstances alone, we can easily be mistaken. The truth may be one hundred and eighty degrees opposite of what you think.

When Paul and Silas were imprisoned, things were progressing *exactly* the way God wanted them to. I don't mean that God wanted their backs beaten, but He sent them there to overcome every circumstance, and overcome they did.

Nothing he experienced ever prevented Paul from doing what he was sent to do, for he was committed to the defense of the Gospel. No matter what discouraging circumstance he faced, he never changed his mind or retreated.

So, much like Paul and Silas, the church in Smyrna was experiencing persecution for having been right in the center of God's will. These believers were walking in the light that they had received. The Lord is pleased with people like that, and He has no rebuke for them. This is one of the two churches addressed in Revelation 2 and 3 that the Lord had no rebuke for.

A Word for Overcomers

"Fear none of those things which thou shalt suffer," Jesus says. Don't be afraid of what the devil has tried to do, because you will overcome in Christ.

"Ye shall have tribulation ten days [notice this is a limited period of time]: be thou faithful unto death, and I will give thee a crown of life."

Hasn't Jesus already done that? Aren't you wearing a crown of life right now because of Jesus; because of the Holy Ghost in your life; because of the Word of God? Yes, you are. But there is *an ultimate reward* that comes to you in heaven because of faithfulness in this life, and this is what Jesus is referring to.

Jesus is talking to an overcomer. Let's study this passage from that point of view. You wear a crown of life both now (in this life) and *then* (in heaven).

You overcome now, so you have that crown of life now. You're wearing it now. As you speak the Word of God, it's because you are a king and a priest now. Kings wear crowns, don't they? You wear the crown of life.

Jesus wore the crown of thorns so that you can wear the crown of life! And He didn't mean for you to wait until you get to heaven to put it on.

Overcoming Tribulation

We come to something else now: tribulation. Didn't Jesus Himself say in John 16:33, ". . . in the world ye shall have tribulation: but. . . ." But what? "Be of good cheer; I have overcome the world." If you know that, and you know you're in Him, then you know you will overcome.

That doesn't mean you won't experience persecution. You *will*. It comes with the package! "Yea, and all that will live godly in Christ Jesus shall suffer persecution," Paul teaches in Second Timothy 3:12. Jesus is telling us the same thing in a different way here in Revelation 2. He is saying that He has given us the crown of life that causes us to overcome in all situations.

Spiritual Death

Jesus resumes His letter in verse 11: "He that hath an ear, let him hear what the Spirit saith unto the churches; He that overcometh shall not be hurt of the second death."

Jesus is looking ahead to Revelation 20, where we see the great White Throne Judgment, and we find that the second death is a final decision from which there is no appeal.

Did you know that *spiritual death* happens to every person in this life? Paul says in Romans 7, "I was alive without the law once: but when the commandment came, sin revived and, [what?] I died" (v. 9). *This means that Paul died spiritually!* He became spiritually separated from God because he coveted willfully, with the full knowledge that covetousness was sin.

Obviously, Paul did not die *naturally*, because he was writing this epistle to the Romans! Even though he died spiritually and was separated from God, he came back to life, or he was born again, when He accepted Jesus Christ as his Lord and Savior, didn't he?

This is true: *You can overcome spiritual death while you're living in this world.* Every human being who is born into this world has the ability and the privilege to overcome spiritual death by accepting Jesus Christ as their Lord and Savior?

However, it is also true that *you cannot overcome the second death.* That's the final separation of all people who have rejected God, and specifically Jesus Christ, God's way of salvation. They rejected the opportunity that God held out to them by His right hand — the opportunity to accept His Son Jesus Christ while they were in this life.

So this passage of scripture refers to the time when that great White Throne Judgment will occur; the time when all persons who have rejected Jesus are ultimately separated forever from God. And Jesus says you will not be hurt by that. Why? Because you won't be appearing at the great White Throne!

We Christians won't be judged at the great White Throne. There is a separate judgment in heaven for believers. In this judgment, the Judgment Seat of Christ, we will be judged by what we did with what God gave us in this life. In other words, we will be judged by what we did, how obedient we were, how faithful we were, and so forth.

The Rewards of Faithfulness

If you go out and do what God told you to do, even if no one responds, you'll have a reward for it. (I don't mean to imply that no one will respond to your ministry, but sometimes it may look that way!) Just do what God tells you to do — that's all God asks. The rest is up to Him. Jesus said He would build the Church; He didn't say you would. You'll see Him do it right before your eyes!

So be faithful. Keep on doing what God told you to do. Even if the people never respond, you will still have a reward — you will still have stars in your crown — because of your faithfulness.

The Second Death

Jesus promises in verse 10, "He that overcometh shall not be hurt of the second death." Since you're not going to be judged at the great White Throne, how could you possibly be hurt by the second death?

Let's look at it the way God sees it: Did God prepare hell for mankind? No, He prepared it for the devil and his fallen angels. The Bible plainly states that the Lord is ". . . not willing that any should perish, but that all should come to repentance" (2 Peter 3:9). Isn't that right? *That's* the will of God for mankind, isn't it?

So does God *desire* to see any one in hell? No. Is He going to *rejoice* over anyone going there? What is His view of hell? We'll find our answers in Ezekiel 33:11:

> **Say unto them, As I live, saith the Lord God, I have no pleasure in the death of the wicked; but that the wicked turn from his way and live: turn ye, turn ye from your evil ways; for why will ye die, O house of Israel?**

God has no pleasure in the death of the wicked. No pleasure. None. If it is grievous to God, what would it be to you and me? The same. We're His children, aren't we? So if we had to witness people being judged and forever separated from God because we failed somehow to be faithful, it would devastate us, wouldn't it?

However, when that White Throne Judgment occurs, there will be no grievous effect on believers at all if we have overcome — if we were faithful in this life.

The important thing is to keep on overcoming. Continue to be faithful. Walk with God and keep your sins under the blood of the Lord Jesus Christ.

If you have confessed your sins to God in this lifetime, He won't bring them up to you at the Judgment Seat of Christ. He won't say, "Why did you do this or why didn't you do that?" No! He said He would never even touch them again with His remembrance.

Therefore, at the great White Throne Judgment, if you have walked in the light you have, and if you continue to walk in the light, you'll not be hurt in any way by the second death.

Chapter 3
The Church in Pergamos

And to the angel of the church in Pergamos write;
These things saith he which hath the sharp sword with
two edges;

I know thy works, and where thou dwellest, even
where Satan's seat is: and thou holdest fast my name
and hast not denied my faith, even in those days
wherein Antipas was my faithful martyr, who was
slain among you, where Satan dwelleth.

But I have a few things against thee, because thou
hast there them that hold the doctrine of Balaam, who
taught Balac to cast a stumblingblock before the
children of Israel, to eat things sacrificed unto idols,
and to commit fornication.

So hast thou also them that hold the doctrine of
the Nicolaitanes, which thing I hate.

Repent; or else I will come unto thee quickly, and
will fight against them with the sword of my mouth.

He that hath an ear, let him hear what the Spirit
saith unto the churches; To him that overcometh will
I give to eat of the hidden manna, and will give him
a white stone, and in the stone a new name written,
which no man knoweth saving he that receiveth it.

Revelation 2:12-17

Historical and Geographical Background

The ancient capital of Asia was Pergamos. An
unusual city, built upon a cone-shaped mountain

fifteen miles inland from the sea, Pergamos, or Pergamum, as it is also referred to, was the cultural center of Asia.

Pergamos boasted a great library, second only to the fabled library of Alexandria, Egypt. This library contained more than 200,000 rolls of papyrus and parchment. The parchment itself, made of dried animal skins, was invented in Pergamum and later supplanted Egyptian papyrus as the preferred writing material of that time.

This city on a high hill on the Caicus River Valley is referred to in John's Revelation as the "seat of Satan." This is no doubt a reference to the fact that Roman emperor worship was very strong in Pergamos, as it was in Smyrna and Ephesus.

Other Greek gods had been worshipped here in earlier times. Although their temples and altars remained, that worship had waned, except for the worship of Asclepios, who supposedly was the god of healing. His temples were the nearest thing to hospitals that the early world knew.

Galen, an early physician, practiced the medicine of that day here and made some advances in the natural treatment of human ills.

Some referred to Asclepios as Asclepios Soter, or "Asclepios the Savior." Christians were especially repulsed by such a use of the name "savior," and would not use the term in such a way. However, it was the worship of the Roman emperor and the Christians' refusal to call Caesar "Lord" which brought forth the greatest persecutions against believers, sometimes ending in their martyrdom.

The modern city of Bergama, with a population of 40,000, stands near the site of ancient Pergamos.

The Twoedged Sword

What is this sharp sword with two edges that is mentioned in verse 12? It's God's Word. God's Word brings both *blessing* and *judgment*.

God's Word has already been spoken. If people get in line with it, it brings them the blessings of God. If they oppose it, they bring the judgment of God's Word upon their life.

It's like a little child who asks, "Why are you spanking me?"

"Because you disobeyed me."

"Well, why do you have to spank me?"

"Because I told you to obey me, and you disobeyed me. You brought it on yourself."

Teach your children that. Teach them individual responsibility. Teach them to be responsible for themselves. I should hope you're not spanking them because you're mad at them; your motive in spanking them should be because you love them.

You punish them because they broke your rule; your command to them. It's when authority has been broken that the child should be punished. When authority has been challenged directly, they have to find out that there is something backing it up — not empty or idle words.

Some parents threaten, "Johnny, you stop that, or I'm going to spank you!" But they never do it.

Don't say that. When your child breaks your commandment, just go get the rod. You won't have to say a thing; Johnny will know what you're going to do next!

It's very easy to get into this habit of saying to your children, "If you don't quit that, I'm going to get on your case!" That idle threat goes on and on, and you never do get on their case.

What have you taught them? *You've taught them that you don't mean what you say!* Is that what you *want* to teach your children? Teach them by your consistent care for them.

Show them what God is like! It will help them know God!

If we know God, we know that He is consistent in much the same way. He will be merciful forever, but all His ways are judgment. Love exacts the penalty when our own works of the flesh have brought that penalty due.

Satan's Seat

Verse 13 begins, "I know thy works, and where thou dwellest, even where Satan's seat is...." This church is right in the midst of a great deal of demonic activity. There are parts of the world like that. There are even parts of the United States like that.

I used to live in Northern California, and the devil had some churches in San Francisco. These were out-and-out satanic churches, with priests of Satan who worshipped the devil and evil spirits. They brought forth many evil manifestations in that city.

Some nations are even worse than that. There are places where the Gospel of the Lord Jesus Christ has not been heard or believed. You can readily see the results of it by the terrible bondage those people live in.

Regaining Your First Love

Remember that Jesus told the church in Ephesus that they had left their first love. Your first dependence and your first responsive love to what God has done is your first love.

At this point in time, the church in Pergamos has gone beyond that, and Jesus is about to warn them that they have tolerated things they should not have tolerated in their midst. Often judgment comes because of this: The sword of His mouth will fight against them.

Remember, this is a twoedged sword, bestowing both blessing and judgment. So if we agree with God — if we obey God — the blessing is ours. But if we place ourselves in opposition to God or His Word, we bring judgment upon ourselves by our own act.

God's Word will never change. If we don't agree with it, the effect will be judgment upon us.

Faith To Be a Martyr

Verse 13 concludes, ". . .and thou holdest fast my name, and hast not denied my faith, even in those days wherein Antipas was my faithful martyr, who was slain among you, where Satan dwelleth."

Notice that Antipas was a *faithful martyr.* He was martyred because he was faithful. For martyrdom has to do with faith — always, always, always!

Martyrdom is never done against a person's will; martyrdom is something you offer. You *give* your life; it is not *taken* from you.

If your life is stolen from you, that is not martyrdom; it is slaughter. *Martyrdom is always a willing act* — something you do willingly in obedience to God — not because someone steals your life from you.

Antipas ". . .was slain among you, where Satan dwelleth." Some work of the devil — some kind of demonic power — must have been involved, or there would have been no one to *slay* Antipas!

A Call to Martyrdom

Let's look further into what Jesus said about Antipas, the martyr. Some believers have been taught that they should have a long life, and they should live it out. That's true; they should finish their course. God's will is for them to finish it (Hebrews 12:1; 2 Timothy 4:7). However, conditions in every generation are not always the same, and some generations will not have so long to finish their earthly race. Others were not so blessed with the knowledge of God's Word as we are.

God may, in the day in which we live, require that some of us be martyrs. He has done this in other times; especially when strong moves of the Holy Spirit were under way. So if He should require this of some of us in this age, let's learn what true martyrdom is.

We will understand what martyrdom is from studying Hebrews 11, the chapter on the heroes of faith. This entire chapter is a testimony to the faith of the saints, so we can get a good look at what martyrdom is.

Notice how the chapter begins: "Now faith. . . ." In the third verse we see the phrase "through faith." In the fourth verse, it's "by faith." In the fifth verse, "by faith." In the sixth verse, "but without faith," and so on.

Some people would have us think, however, that when we get down to verse 35 that it's *unbelief*. But the whole chapter is a testimony to the *faith* of the saints, so to take this verse out of the chapter and say that martyrdom is the result of unbelief or failure would miss the whole point.

Those who have sat under his teaching, probably have heard Brother Kenneth E. Hagin say that *it takes faith to die.* It's true that death is nothing more than a gateway, but it takes faith to go through it, because you've never been through it before. So no matter how you go out of this life, when you go out through that doorway of death, it takes faith to die.

It's like everything else: The just shall — what? — *live by faith.* They also shall *die by faith,* if they die in the will of God!

After commending all who have shown evidence of their faith, the writer of Hebrews says, starting with verse 33:

> **Who through faith subdued kingdoms, wrought righteousness, obtained promises, stopped the mouths of lions,**

This last phrase refers to Daniel. Daniel had the opportunity to go to be with the Lord prematurely on more than one occasion, didn't he? This verse refers back to Daniel 6, where we find him thrown into a den of ferocious, man-eating lions.

But the angel of God came and stopped the mouths of those lions when Daniel was thrown in with them, and Daniel slept in their midst all night long, probably using one of them for a pillow!

How could Daniel do this? *Because he had faith.* Faith brought God's angel on the scene, and he subdued these lions and stopped their mouths!

A Better Resurrection

> **Quenched the violence of fire, escaped the edge of the sword, out of weakness were made strong, waxed valiant in fight, turned to flight the armies of the aliens.**

Women received their dead raised to life again:
and others were tortured, not accepting deliverance;
that they might obtain a better resurrection:
Hebrews 11:34,35

All of this is by faith, isn't it? It's talking about the faith these people walked in. Their own faith had to be exercised in all these situations.

Notice in verse 35, the martyrs were *offered* deliverance from martyrdom, but they refused to *accept* deliverance. Did they face martyrdom through *unbelief?* No, through *faith!*

The act of laying your life down as a martyr is not the act of someone who is weak in faith; it is the act of someone who is *strong* in faith! In fact, you couldn't do it otherwise — and God would never ask you to do it otherwise.

These martyrs chose not to accept deliverance, desiring to obtain a better resurrection instead. What is a better resurrection?

Your full obedience is involved. You are obedient unto death; willing to lay your life down if that is something God asks of you, perhaps because He can use it to accomplish His will in the earth.

God promises in Psalm 91 that those who dwell in the secret place of the Most High God shall abide under the shadow, or the protection, of Almighty God. They remain there. And at the end of this famous psalm, God says that He will show His great salvation to those who do, and He will *satisfy them with long life* (v. 16).

Does He now mean to *disappoint you with a short life* by asking you to be a martyr? He can't do both, can He?

In other words, if you're going to lay your life down, you would have to be fully satisfied that you have *fulfilled* your course and race in this world, wouldn't you? If you've got any doubt in your mind about it, would you be able to lay your life down in faith? I don't think so.

The Apostle Paul knew he had finished his race, didn't he? He says so in Second Timothy 4:7, as he writes that last epistle from Rome to Timothy. He says, "I've finished my course. I've finished the race that was set before me, and I'm about to be offered."

Peter knew it, too, didn't he? If you read Second Peter 1:14, you see that he knew he was just about to leave this world. From Early Church historians we know that Peter was crucified upside down. Also, according to reliable Church history, Paul was beheaded. Why would God ask martyrdom of a man like Paul? Paul had already experienced all kinds of persecutions — and he had been delivered from these persecutions more than once. You can read about his deliverance from multiple persecutions in Second Corinthians 11.

Paul knew how to get delivered. He walked in faith, and he knew how to stay alive when everyone wanted him dead. It was not difficult for Paul to escape the edge of the sword. He had done it before. But now, as Paul finishes his course, God asks, "Paul, glorify Me in this way." Why?

Paul was going to have a better resurrection because of his martyrdom. A better resurrection is when there are more people in the resurrection. Hallelujah, martyrdom will always give life to someone!

Jesus became sin for us all, without any comfort. He bore your sickness. He bore your pains of punishment. The Word says literally, "pains of punishment" (Isaiah 53:4), translated here "griefs," from the Hebrew *makob*. Because He bore them, you don't have to bear them. Do you believe that and know it?

The next day, Latimer and his friend were taken out and tied to stakes, and fires were kindled around them. The last that was seen of them, they were singing hymns and praising God. Both of them!

The Result of Martyrdom

That's a testimony. When your enemies can't evoke a cry of pain out of you in the heat of the fire, what's the point? One point is that it is a testimony to their hard hearts, and it will cause some of them to repent.

As we have seen by his own admission, Paul was one of the hard-hearted Pharisees. He was "a Pharisee of the Pharisees" (Acts 23:6), and he was more zealous to persecute the Church than any of his associates.

But *something* turned Paul's life around. *Something* convinced him that these believers in Jesus of Nazareth had what he lacked. I suspect it was the response of the people he persecuted — not just Stephen alone, but the others, too.

We saw in verse 35 of our text that others were tortured, but they would not accept deliverance. Deliverance was there for them — they could have had it. They'd been delivered many times before, so why didn't they accept it this time?

Because they knew from God that it was His will for them to lay their life down, and they were willing to do it. Now that's martyrdom! Anything less than that is not true martyrdom; it would be more like loss or slaughter.

Christians have been slaughtered in many places — even in recent history. I'm thinking of Uganda. A few years ago, Idi Amin became dictator of that nation, and he began to systematically slaughter the Christians in Uganda.

Some of them escaped to tell the tale. The rivers of Uganda literally ran red with the blood of those killed — hundreds of thousands of them — for Amin's troops threw their bodies into the rivers.

Why did the church get slaughtered in Uganda? Because it was a baby church — it wasn't a mature church — and because they didn't know how to spiritually resist such severe persecution.

It is not God's will for a whole nation — a whole church in a nation — to be exterminated. Think about it: Could that ever be God's will? Of course not.

It could be the will of God for a mature saint who is ready to go home anyway. Some "mature" saints are younger in years than others, so it wouldn't necessarily be a gray-headed saint who was ready for martyrdom; it would be someone who had finished his course.

Aren't You Promised a Long Life?

Jesus finished his course in thirty-three years. You could do the same if you really wanted to. You needn't look at that promised seventy or eighty years in Psalm 90:10 as being the limit of life. If you read the context, I believe it's talking about the ones who didn't believe God. They died in the wilderness at seventy years of age, and by reason of natural strength, some of them lasted eighty years.

But how long did Moses live? One hundred and twenty years. How long did Joshua live? One hundred and seventeen years. Caleb was older than Joshua when he died. Aaron, Moses' brother, lived to be one hundred and twenty-three. Miriam, their sister, died at one hundred and twenty-four.

People who believed God didn't die at seventy or eighty years of age! Why should we settle for that? Read Psalm 90 in its context. It does not state that we ought to die at seventy or eighty; it says that the people who didn't believe God died at these ages.

So you see, I'm not trying to talk you out of believing God for a long life. You've got to be satisfied with the length of your life. To be a martyr, you've got to know that you've finished your course, and that God's purpose for your life is fulfilled in order to seemingly cut your life short.

This is because God can't go against His Word. He promises us long life. The first commandment with promise is Exodus 20:12, where God instructed the Israelites, "Honour thy father and thy mother: that thy days may be long upon the land which the Lord thy God giveth thee."

The Doctrine of Balaam

Returning to Revelation 2:13, we see that Antipas was a faithful martyr — a person who laid his life down willingly. His faithful death produced fruit in other people's lives. After commending Antipas, Jesus turns His attention to the church in Pergamos and says in verse 14:

> But I have a few things against thee, because thou hast there them that hold the doctrine of Balaam, who taught Balac to cast a stumblingblock before the

44

children of Israel, to eat things sacrificed unto idols, and to commit fornication.

Balaam was a prophet of God, wasn't he? Yes, he was. Whenever he opened his mouth by the anointing, he spoke wonderful things. (Read them in Numbers 22.) But Balaam was persuaded by the lust of his flesh — by greed, you might say — to use his office to get himself gain.

First of all, Balac, the King of Moab, was concerned about the Israelites coming up out of Egypt. He looked out and saw this great multitude of people, and he was afraid of them.

As you may recall, Moab and Ammon were the cousins of Israel. They knew about Israel. They knew the history of Jacob and Esau, and so forth. They knew what the prophets had foretold that Israel would become a great nation.

God's in the multiplying business. Seventy Israelites went down to Egypt, and about four hundred years later about three million of them came out! So when Balac saw this great number of them coming into his country, he hired Balaam, who was a prophet of God.

Balaam probably was a descendant of Esau. You can't prove it, but you can see it fairly well from the places he lived and the names of his relatives. And Balac hired him to curse Israel!

At first, Balaam wanted the reward that was offered by the king, but God said, "No, don't take it." Now, if Balaam had been smart, that would have been the end of it right there, but he kept pushing. *He wanted the reward the king offered more than he wanted to be obedient to God, who made him a prophet.*

Balaam was enough of a prophet, however, to know when God was speaking through him and when He wasn't. Finally he went to see Balac. Balac took him up on a mountaintop and showed him what was happening in his kingdom: Israel was coming through the land of Moab. And Balac said, "Now curse them for me!"

So Balac built altars for the prophet, but when it came time to curse the Israelites, there was no word from God against Israel: He couldn't find one. Balaam knew that he couldn't "manufacture" one, so he wouldn't curse Israel.

He and the king went through this charade a few more times, with the same result each time: God wouldn't anoint the prophet to say anything against Israel.

How To Get God Mad

But the prophet *still* wanted the reward. Since he couldn't prophesy against the Israelites, what did he do to get the reward? He knew something from the knowledge of God about the Israelites, and he used this knowledge to get himself gain: He taught the King of Moab how to corrupt Israel!

Balaam said, "There's no word from God against them, but if you'll send your daughters down there and place your idols in their midst, commit fornication, and teach them to worship idols, God will judge them." (See Revelation 2:14; Numbers 25.)

The King of Moab followed his advice. Judgment in the form of a great plague fell upon the camp because of Israel's disobedience. Phinehas, the grandson of Aaron, ran out in the middle of the camp, took zealous corrective action, and the plague was stayed — but not before twenty-four thousand people died. (See Numbers 25:6-9.)

Now you can understand what the doctrine of Balaam is: *The doctrine of Balaam is to do whatever it takes to get what you want — to use whatever God gave you to get yourself gain.*

Now Jesus is telling the church in Pergamos, "I have a few things against thee, because thou hast there them that hold the doctrine of Balaam, who taught Balac to cast a stumblingblock before the children of Israel, to eat things sacrificed unto idols, and to commit fornication."

Jesus is warning the church of Pergamos against tolerating such things, isn't He? And if He were here today, writing to the modern Church, He'd be telling us the same thing: "Don't tolerate that in your midst!" He continues in verse 15:

> **So hast thou also them that hold the doctrine of the Nicolaitanes, which I hate.**

"Don't tolerate the deeds of the Nicolaitanes." We've already discussed that. They were loose and careless in the way they lived in the natural, and they elevated the clergy or ministers above the people they ministered to.

You know, there really isn't any rank in the Body of Christ. Yes, there are "offices" — positions people are called to — and we ought to give honor to and submit to the people in those "offices," but we are all brothers and sisters. Their "office" doesn't make them any better than anyone else. They don't outrank anyone else. We've all been washed in the same blood — the blood of Jesus Christ! We have thereby all been made members of one Body.

Jesus continues His message in verse 16:

Repent; or else I will come unto thee quickly, and will fight against them with the sword of my mouth.

Again, the church at Pergamos is told what to do about things that need to be corrected: "Don't tolerate these things any longer in your midst. Don't tolerate things you know are immoral or wrong. Correct them, but correct them with the right spirit and the right attitude."

How To Correct Those in Error

The Bible way to correct fellow believers is found in Galatians 6. I recognize that there is some difference between what we've been reading in Revelation and this passage, but if mature Christians would go to their fellow believers when they first saw signs of a problem, the weaker believers would never get to the point that Balaam did.

The chapter starts out, "Brethren. . . ." Who is Paul writing to? The Church! ". . . if a man be overtaken in a fault, ye which are spiritual, restore such an one in the spirit of meekness; considering thyself, lest thou also be tempted. Bear ye one another's burdens, and so fulfill the law of Christ" (Galatians 6:1,2).

You might protest, "We would never have that kind of problem!" Anyplace can! You who recognize the problem — you who see clearly — you who are seeing in the Spirit — are to restore your fellow believer in the spirit of meekness.

The person who is having the problem obviously isn't seeing clearly in the Spirit, is he? If he's been *overtaken* in a fault, he's not seeing clearly in the Spirit. He's not walking in the Spirit; he's walking in the realm of the flesh, and perhaps the devil's having a heyday with him!

Here's what Paul tells you who see the situation clearly — you who know what's going on — to do: *"Restore such a person!"* Restore him — don't cast him out!

However, if he doesn't respond to the love of God that is manifest to him through those who go to him, eventually it may be necessary for him to be separated from the company of believers. You can see that from other testimonies of scripture, but that's not where we start.

I've been around some Charismatic groups that were overzealous. The minute people did something wrong, "Out with them! Throw them out!" But that's not the will or the purpose of God in such cases.

Your Role in Correction

The Holy Spirit, through Paul, instructed, "If you see someone overtaken in a fault, you who see it clearly go to him and restore him to the walk in the Spirit — and do it *in the spirit of meekness!*"

That means to be humble; to be dependent upon God; to be looking to the leadership of the Holy Spirit; and to consider yourself, realizing that you will probably learn something from the situation as well. We *will* learn something from such experiences if we approach them with the right kind of attitude. We will be just as benefitted as the person we went to help.

What is the right attitude? Being teachable. Being dependent upon God. "Considering thyself, lest thou also be tempted."

That's the way we should go to people who are exhibiting problems. We shouldn't sit and wait until the problem becomes a full-blown festering cancer that's eating half the church before we do something about it.

Those in a leadership position should not wait when you see such things happening. Don't say, "Well, I'll just pray about it and see what God can do." No, when you see something that needs to be corrected, it's *your* responsibility as a leader of the church to go and approach that person.

There's no time to say, "Well, it will take care of itself." If you ignore it and hope it goes away, it won't. "Well, it's not my business what they do." Yes, it is your business if you're a shepherd of the sheep.

By this I don't mean you are to meddle in other people's *private* lives. Galatians 6 is discussing *spiritual* matters that should be self-evident to you who are spiritual. You will recognize and know these things by natural fact or by the Holy Spirit. Do not allow such things to fester in your midst.

Promises to Overcomers

Jesus completes His message to the church at Pergamos in verse 17:

> **He that hath an ear, let him hear what the Spirit saith unto the churches: To him that overcometh will I give to eat of the hidden manna, and will give him a white stone, and in the stone a new name written, which no man knoweth saving he that receiveth it.**

Let's look at that phrase "to him that overcometh." I'm an overcomer by the blood of the Lamb and by the word of my testimony, it says in Revelation 12:11.

> **And they overcame him by the blood of the Lamb, and by the word of their testimony; and they loved not their lives unto the death.**

I'll finish my course. I'll run my race. I'll have a full reward! Praise God, that's the full reward of the overcomer (v. 14). We can see that we're overcoming now, and that there is an ultimate, final result of it.

What is "the hidden manna"? What was manna in the Old Testament? It was *food*, wasn't it? It was like coriander seed. It was what sustained the Israelites in the wilderness. And it was very much what? *Supernatural*. It fell out of heaven for them each day!

Each person was to gather as much as he or she wanted to eat that day. Then, on the day *before* the Sabbath, they were allowed to gather for both days. But if they gathered a two-day supply any other day, the manna would rot and stink. They weren't supposed to store it.

So *manna is what God sustained their life with supernaturally during their journey in the wilderness.* All right, *the hidden manna is just that: It's the Word of God!* It's what God feeds us with supernaturally.

He is what He sustains us with! The Word of God is what He causes us to grow by. According to John 3:21, ". . .he that doeth the truth cometh to the light. . . ." In other words, the person who is a doer of the Word is enlightened further by that Word.

Another promise Jesus made to overcomers in verse 17 of our text is, "I will give him a white stone." *A white stone was a symbol of being acquitted!*

Whenever there was a trial in those times, the judge had two stones: a white stone and a black stone. One or the other was rendered as a verdict.

We will receive a white stone because we are not guilty; we have been acquitted. Look at Romans 8:1: "There is therefore now no condemnation to them

Chapter 4
The Church in Thyatira

And unto the angel of the church in Thyatira write; These things saith the Son of God, who hath his eyes like unto a flame of fire, and his feet are like fine brass;

I know thy works, and charity, and service, and faith, and thy patience, and thy works; and the last to be more than the first.

Notwithstanding I have a few things against thee, because thou sufferest that woman Jezebel, which calleth herself a prophetess, to teach and to seduce my servants to commit fornication, and to eat things sacrificed unto idols.

And I gave her space to repent of her fornication; and she repented not.

Behold, I will cast her into a bed, and them that commit adultery with her into great tribulation, except they repent of their deeds.

And I will kill her children with death; and all the churches shall know that I am he which searcheth the reins and hearts: and I will give unto every one of you according to your works.

But unto you I say, and unto the rest in Thyatira, as many as have not this doctrine, and which have not known the depths of Satan, as they speak; I will put upon you none other burden.

But that which ye have already hold fast till I come.

And he that overcometh, and keepeth my works unto the end, to him will I give power over the nations.

And he shall rule them with a rod of iron, as the vessels of a potter shall they be broken to shivers: even as I received of my Father.

And I will give him the morning star.

He that hath an ear, let him hear what the Spirit saith unto the churches.

Revelation 2:18-29

Historical and Geographical Background

Thyatira was the smallest and least significant of all the seven Asian cities addressed in Revelation. Very little is known of its history, compared with the other six cities addressed.

Thyatira was located on the Lycus River, midway between Pergamos and Sardis. The wool and dye trades were very strong in Thyatira; in fact, the city's tradesmen and craftsmen were highly organized into many labor and trade guilds, the counterpart of modern unions.

Great pressure was put on all tradesmen and craftsmen to join and participate in the sometimes pagan activities of these guilds.

Christians in this region found it nearly impossible to belong to the guilds without violating their conscience. This presented an urgent and difficult dilemma, for without guild membership, there was no work available.

Lydia, "the seller of purple" who is referred to in Acts 16:13-15, was from Thyatira. This "purple" was a peculiarly dyed cloth produced in the Thyatira region which was in great demand in the world of that day.

Therefore, it was also very expensive and was used to make the finest of garments and draperies.

The modern Turkish city of Akahsar, with a population of some 60,000 people, stands on the site of the ancient city. Wool and dyes are still a major industry in that region.

This letter to the church in Thyatira, strangely enough, was the longest and most instructive of all the seven written in Revelation. From this we must deduce that what was happening in the church in that place was and is *very important* to the life of the Church, both then and now.

Weaknesses and Strengths

Verse 18 of our text notes that the Son of God has "eyes like unto a flame of fire." This shows Jesus Christ's omniscience — it means He is all-knowing. ". . .and his feet are like fine brass." This means that Jesus Christ, the son of man, the Word of God, judges things that are not in agreement with Him. He will bring all things into either a willing self-judgment through the Word, or an eternal separation for those who reject the Gospel.

And judgment begins where? At the house of God (First Peter 4:17). We are to judge ourselves, aren't we? God has permitted us to do that. He permits us to judge ourselves because He is confident in the work of His Word and in the work of the Holy Spirit in us. If God is confident in this, then we can be confident in it, too.

You may ask, "What if I don't measure up to what someone else does?" Don't measure yourself by someone else; measure yourself by what you know of the Word of God.

your assurance as a minister of the Gospel, among other things. But don't let Satan do this to you! Hold fast to what you have!

The Dangers of Immorality

At this point in these seven letters, we have seen four specific warnings concerning sexual immorality in the Church.

No other one sin, when tolerated or allowed, so weakens the Church and leads it in a downward spiral! It opens the door to greater and greater problems.

The Jesus Movement among street people and Hippies was a powerful and mighty move of God by His Spirit in the 1960s. That movement, however, waned and stagnated primarily because not enough strong moral leadership was provided to reverse the trends and tendencies that existed in those people's lives.

There were some ministries in those times and places that insisted on godly living and succeeded in attaining it, but they were too few and far between. Today we are faced with sexual immorality within the Church.

The success of the Church in answering our Great Commission will be in direct proportion to how faithfully we deal with that same immorality that always tries to gain a foothold in our midst.

> **And he that overcometh, and keepeth my works unto the end, to him will I give power over the nations:**
>
> **And he shall rule them with a rod of iron; as the vessels of a potter shall they be broken to shivers, even as I received of my Father.**
>
> **And I will give him the morning star.**
> **Revelation 2:26-28**

This all refers to authority and the position of a believer in relation to this world we're living in. Ultimately, yes, we will reign with Christ in the Millennial Kingdom. Literally, we will reign over this world.

Our Authority in This World

Even now you have authority over the nations. But what do you have authority *to do* over the nations? *Fulfill the Great Commission!* That's what Jesus gave us the authority to do when He was about to ascend up into heaven:

> And he said unto them, Go ye into all the world, and preach the gospel to every creature.
>
> He that believeth and is baptized shall be saved, but he that believeth not shall be damned.
>
> And these signs shall follow them that believe; In my name shall they cast out devils; They shall speak with new tongues;
>
> They shall take up serpents; and if they drink any deadly thing, it shall not hurt them; they shall lay hands on the sick, and they shall recover.
>
> **Mark 16:15-18**

That's what we have authority to do. *That's* what we're here to do. We're not responsible to turn the world into paradise before Jesus comes; we're here to preach the Gospel and win everyone who will come out of the world — the ones God has long patience for. That's what we're here to do now.

Jesus said to the church of Thyatira that he would give those who overcome power over the nations. This really means authority, so you have authority to do what the Great Commission says.

What are we told to do in First Timothy 2? Pray "For kings, and for all that are in authority; that we may lead a quiet and peaceable life in all godliness and honesty" (v. 2). And when we do that, what will happen? We will live a quiet and peaceable life, the Word says. What do peaceful circumstances give us the opportunity to do? Go and preach!

It's hard to go preach when wars are going on! You can hardly expect people to come to a meeting when bombs are exploding everywhere! So we need to pray. That's our responsibility. Jesus gave us that authority, didn't He, by His Word? If we fail to do it, what's going to happen? The world will be in a chaotic situation.

Believing Prayer Gets Results

But if we pray, what will happen? Believing prayers of intercession in 1983 turned an attempted coup in Kenya that was succeeding into disorganized chaos, thus allowing the legally constituted government of that nation to return to power.

It also allowed the church of the Lord Jesus Christ in that nation to remain strong and continue to be a vital witness in our time in Africa.

An African bishop of a church in Kenya told me firsthand of how he and another believer prayed on behalf of Kenya's president and how the conspirators actually eliminated each other within hours after the Christians had prayed.

Yes, we can have power over nations now — over their situations and over their destinies!

When I was teaching a Sunday School class once, the Lord impressed me to have us pray for the country of Lebanon. We found where the Word said Lebanon would be "a fruitful field" (Isaiah 29:17-20). Although that shattered land has been everything *but* a fruitful field for the last ten years, God will turn the situation around. God wants those of us who know this promise to pray that it will come to pass.

Pray "For kings, and for all that are in authority; that we may lead a quiet and peaceable life...For this is good and acceptable in the sight of God our Saviour; Who will have all men to be saved, and to come unto the knowledge of the truth..." (vv. 2-4). That's the will of God.

Not everyone will be saved, but everyone will have the opportunity to be saved through hearing the Gospel preached. Not everyone will accept salvation, but don't underestimate how many will.

The Bright and Morning Star

The Lord has given *us* authority and power over the nations. In verses 27 and 28, He says "And he shall rule them "with a rod of iron; as the vessels of a potter shall they be broken to shivers: even as I received of my Father. And I will give him the morning star."

Jesus said in Revelation 22:16, "I am the bright and morning star." Once Jesus called another being — Lucifer — a "morning star," and "day star." Before Lucifer fell from heaven, he was called that (Isaiah 14:12 NAS, AMP). But Jesus has called you and me that, too! He also said, "Ye are the light of the world" (Matthew 5:14).

The morning star is a source of light. It's brighter than the sun! You can see it in the morning sky when the sun's up. You can't see the rest of the stars, but you can see that one.

So this passage is a picture of you having authority now over the nations to fulfill the Great Commission and eventually to rule in totality over all the nations in the next age.

Chapter 2 concludes with a statement that is repeated over and over again after every letter: "He that hath an ear, let him hear what the Spirit saith unto the churches" (v. 29).

"He that hath an ear" is a man or woman who has spiritual understanding. Let this person hear how and what the Spirit is correcting, guiding, leading, commending, warning, and promising.

People with spiritual understanding are not only going to *hear* these words; they are going to *do* these things. That's what Jesus is really saying: "*Do* what you're hearing. *Apply* the Word of God to your life."

Chapter 5
The Church in Sardis

And unto the angel of the church in Sardis write, These things saith he that hath the seven Spirits of God, and the seven stars; I know thy works, that thou hast a name that thou livest, and art dead.

Be watchful, and strengthen the things which remain, that are ready to die: for I have not found thy works perfect before God.

Remember, therefore how thou hast received and heard, and hold fast, and repent. If therefore thou shalt not watch, I will come on thee as a thief, and thou shalt not know what hour I will come upon thee.

Thou hast a few names even in Sardis which have not defiled their garments; and they shall walk with me in white: for they are worthy.

He that overcometh, the same shall be clothed in white raiment; and I will not blot out his name out of the book of life, but I will confess his name before my Father, and before his angels.

He that hath an ear, let him hear what the Spirit saith unto the churches.

Revelation 3:1-6

Historical and Geographical Background

The city of Sardis was once the wealthiest and most splendid city in all Asia. The ancient Lydian capital had been the seat of Croesus, the richest king of the sixth century B.C. When the Persian king, Cyrus the

I often take First Thessalonians 5:12-22 as a check-up list. Notice I didn't use the word "check list." I use these verses to evaluate and reprove myself from time to time: "And we beseech you brethren...." If I am honest with myself, this will be a safe barometer of my spiritual condition at any given moment.

This church in Sardis needed to be more watchful and diligent. As they had been overcome in natural warfare on two occasions through carelessness and overconfidence, they were warned that spiritual disaster was awaiting them unless they repented.

That is simply because sins of commission or omission are continuing to eat away at the will and eventually the spiritual life of those who tolerate such acts of darkness and disobedience.

Doers of the Word

In verse 3, Jesus said, "Remember therefore how thou hast received and heard...." Well, how did we receive, and how did we hear? Faith comes by hearing. Hearing what? The Word of God! And we receive it in its fullness by applying it in our life; by being a doer of it. And we know that "...he that doeth truth cometh to the light..." (John 3:21).

So here we've got a picture of the importance of being doers of what we hear. Jesus told the believers in Sardis that they must remember what they heard, hold fast, and repent; otherwise, He must come upon them as a thief in the night.

He concludes His letter by saying:

> Thou hast a few names even in Sardis which have not defiled their garments; and they shall walk with me in white: for they are worthy.

> He that overcometh, the same shall be clothed in white raiment; and I will not blot out his name out of the book of life, but I will confess his name before my Father, and before his angels.
>
> He that hath an ear, let him hear what the Spirit saith unto the churches.
>
> Revelation 3:4-6

What did Jesus say in Matthew 10:32? "Whosoever therefore shall confess me before men, him will I confess before my Father which is in heaven."

That's both *now* and in the *hereafter*. However, there is a very serious warning given here to those who refuse to overcome sin; to those who tolerate works of darkness in their lives.

Jesus said of the overcomer, "I will not blot out his name out of the book of life." Ask yourself this question: What will He do in the case of the person who has reindulged himself in a lifestyle of sin and refuses to repent or overcome that sinful lifestyle?

Such an act of denial of Jesus Christ could only come at the end of a long path of backsliding and presumptuous sinning. Why, then, should we, the blood-washed believers, take even the first step in that direction? We shouldn't — and by the grace of God we won't.

Historical and Geographical Background

The city of Philadelphia was the youngest of all the seven cities. It had been founded by colonists from Pergamos around 150 B.C.

The new colony was named after Attalus the Second, King of Pergamos. This king's strong love for his own brother, Eumenes, had earned him the new name of Philadelphos, or "one who loves his brother."

Philadelphia was founded with the express purpose of being a missionary of Greek culture and language to the older nations of Lydia and Phrygia. It did its job so well that by A.D. 19, the Lydians had forgotten their own language and culture, and were all but Greeks.

This was a foreshadowing of the church that would come into existence there in the latter half of the first century and reach out into those same regions with the Gospel of the Lord Jesus Christ.

Of all the churches addressed in Revelation, this is the only one still alive today. The modern city of Alasehir, population 20,000, still has a Christian bishop and more than 1000 practicing Christians within that community.

Situated on the east side of the Tmolus mountains in the valley of the Cogamis River, this city and its church have overcome the wave of Mohammedanism and survived as a free Christian city when all others were falling to Islam and the Turks around A.D. 1300.

This is a wonderful testimony to a church that Jesus had no rebuke, but only commendation, for. It stands today to prove that the Word of God is true. What better testimonial to Deuteronomy 7:9:

"Know therefore that the Lord thy God, he is God, the faithful God, which keepeth covenant and mercy with them that love him and keep his commandments to a thousand generations."

The Philadelphian church had an open door set before them by God which no man could close. That door of utterance for the Gospel of Jesus Christ is still open there today. Praise the Lord!

No Rebuke for the Philadelphians

Did you notice that Jesus had no rebuke for the Philadelphians? He didn't warn them about anything. Why not? There's a simple answer to that: *They were walking in the light they had received from God.* That's all God asks.

Notice, too, that Jesus didn't say they were great and powerful in faith; He said they had a little faith — but they were walking in the light they had; they were being doers of what they heard.

There are a number of things that are interesting to us in this letter. For example, look back in Second Samuel 8, beginning with the first verse.

> And after this it came to pass, that David smote the Philistines, and subdued them: and David took Methegammah out of the hand of the Philistines.
>
> And he smote Moab, and measured them with a line, casting them down to the ground; even with two lines measured he to put to death, and with one full line to keep alive. And so the Moabites became David's servants, and brought gifts.
>
> David smote also Hadadezer, the son of Rehob, king of Zobah, as he went to recover his border at the river Euphrates.
>
> And David took from him a thousand chariots, and seven hundred horsemen, and twenty thousand

footmen: and David houghed all the chariot horses,
[that means he cut the major muscles in their legs] **but reserved of them for an hundred chariots.**

And when the Syrians of Damascus came to succour Hadadezer king of Zobah, David slew of the Syrians two and twenty thousand men.

Then David put garrisons in Syria of Damascus: and the Syrians became servants to David, and brought gifts. And the Lord preserved David whithersoever he went.

2 Samuel 8:1-6

It says again in the fourteenth verse, "And the Lord preserved David whithersoever he went." This passage tells how David overcame Edom, Ammon, Syria, and Moab, the nations that surrounded Israel. Israel was and still is surrounded by enemies except on one side: the ocean. On all other sides, Israel is ringed by her enemies.

Until David became king, those hostile nations took turns harassing Israel whatever way they wanted to. When Israel was strong in the Lord, they didn't do it. But whenever the children of Israel were disobedient, these enemies and others took turns invading the country, and doing whatever they wanted to with it and its inhabitants.

But when David became king, he defeated every enemy. Not just *some* of their enemies — *all* of them! And the country enjoyed peace and rest even throughout his son Solomon's 40-year reign. No one dared mess with them. It wasn't because they didn't want to — don't misunderstand that; they did want to, and they still want to — but they didn't do it because they didn't *dare* to do it!

David was that kind of a king. He was a deliverer, a man of war, called for that purpose.

You will recall that Revelation 3:7 said, ". . .These things saith he that is holy, he that is true, he that hath the key of David. . . ." Here Jesus is referring to Himself. He has "the key of David."

Keys symbolize control and authority. If you have the keys to doors, you can lock them or open them; you can open them or shut them; you can determine what's open and what's shut. Jesus has the key of David.

All the enemies of God's people have been defeated — not *some* of them; *all* of them — and *they're totally defeated!*

We saw in Second Samuel 8:2 that David ". . .smote Moab, and measured them with a line, casting them down to the ground; even with two lines measured he to put to death, and with one full line to keep alive. And so the Moabites became David's servants, and brought gifts."

There is a passage in First Samuel that tells us that back in the days of Saul, the Moabites came into the land of Israel, as was their custom, in the spring of the year to raid. It was their custom to come into Israel in the spring. They would probably say to one another, "Well, it's springtime; let's go over and raid Israel." And they did it with impunity. They got away with it time after time.

Saul didn't like it, and he tried to stop it, but even he couldn't stop it. But when David came to the throne, it says he measured Moab with a line. He defeated them. He went up against them and defeated them militarily and absolutely.

All the people who survived that defeat he lined up in three lines. The first two lines of people he put of that kind of situation and have left those dead churches. However, we must not forsake those who are unsaved in the formal churches. We must be as prepared to go back and minister to these lost people as we are to minister to lost pagans or heathens.

Next, Jesus promises, "Because thou hast kept the word of my patience, I also will keep thee from the hour of temptation, which shall come upon all the world, to try them that dwell upon the earth" (v. 10).

The Lord is saying to His Body, "Because you have walked in the light and grown, and walked in that increased light of revelation and overcome, and all this continues, *I will keep you from the hour of testing* (a specific time of testing — definitely not testing in general)."

Notice that this temptation or testing will come upon the whole world to try those who still dwell upon the earth. It is the time of Great Tribulation that Jesus taught about in Matthew 24:15-28.

The Word of God just said that believers (overcomers) would be kept *from* that time. It did not say that we would be protected or kept *in* that time. The Church on earth today, and all of the children it spawns in its time, will be in heaven with Jesus when the Great Tribulation occurs.

Then Jesus states, "Behold, I come quickly: hold that fast which thou hast, that no man take thy crown." This Philadelphia Church had crowns of victory and overcoming, crowns of life from their life in Christ Jesus, and they had crowns of reward awaiting them in heaven when they would appear before the Judgment Seat of Christ to receive them.

They are told to hold fast, that no man (being) would take those crowns. To "hold fast" is simply to keep on believing, keep on overcoming, and keep on looking to Jesus, the Author and Finisher of our faith.

The Apostle Paul put it this way: ". . . forgetting those things which are behind, and reaching forth unto those things which are before, I press toward the mark for the prize of the high calling of God in Christ Jesus" (Philippians 3:13,14).

Although the members of the Philadelphia church were not through running the race that was set before them, the Lord was confident that they would finish their course with great joy by continuing the way they were going.

Verse 12: "Him that overcometh will I make a pillar in the temple of my God, and he shall go no more out: and I will write upon him the name of my God, and the name of the city of my God, which is new Jerusalem, which cometh down out of heaven from my God: and I will write upon him my new name."

In this verse, the Lord promises overcomers that the very process of overcoming and growing in the knowledge of God will conform us to the image of Christ (see Romans 8:29-31).

Real eternal security is found in these verses, and is directly related to an overcoming lifestyle. The overcoming believer is changed from glory to glory as he or she beholds God in His Word.

Our identity becomes more and more His; our character becomes more and more His; our will becomes more and more submitted to His.

When the world sees love in God's children, they will know that we are *His* children, and they will believe that He has sent us.

As a paraphrase of verse 13 puts it, "He that has understanding, rest in this knowledge."

Chapter 7
The Church in Laodicea

And unto the angel of the church of the Laodiceans write; These things saith the Amen, the faithful and true witness, the beginning of the creation of God;

I know thy works, that thou art neither cold nor hot: I would thou wert cold or hot.

So then because thou art lukewarm, and neither cold nor hot, I will spue thee out of my mouth.

Because thou sayest, I am rich, and increased with goods, and have need of nothing; and knowest not that thou art wretched, and miserable, and poor, and blind, and naked:

I counsel thee to buy of me gold tried in the fire, that thou mayest be rich; and white raiment, that thou mayest be clothed, and that the shame of thy nakedness do not appear; and anoint thine eyes with eyesalve, that thou mayest see.

As many as I love, I rebuke and chasten: be zealous therefore, and repent.

Behold, I stand at the door, and knock: if any man hear my voice, and open the door, I will come in to him, and will sup with him, and he with me.

To him that overcometh will I grant to sit with me in my throne, even as I also overcame, and am set down with my Father in his throne.

He that hath an ear, let him hear what the Spirit saith unto the churches.

Revelation 3:14-22

83

Historical and Geographical Background

Laodicea was a city on the Lycus River with two other cities, Colossae and Hierapolis, in close proximity. These cities lay approximately 130 miles due east of Ephesus astride the major east-west trade route of that day.

Laodicea had become a center of trade, finance, banking, and investment. The citizens of this city were fabulously wealthy; so much so that when their city was totally destroyed in A.D. 60 by an earthquake, these proud Laodiceans rejected Roman aid offered by the emperor and completely rebuilt that city using their own resources.

The Laodiceans were also noted for their fine woolen garment industry and advances in the medical field pertaining to treatment of eye and ear diseases. Knowing the importance of good natural sight and hearing, it seems incongruous that they were described in this epistle as being without such *spiritual* qualities!

The church in Laodicea was the only church addressed by Jesus Christ without commendation. That means there was *nothing* that He could commend them for.

How is this possible? To paraphrase the Apostle Paul, writing to the church in Galatia, they had begun in the Spirit, but were now gone totally backward into apostasy and the flesh. Some may not believe this to be possible, but the evidence of this epistle is that Jesus *could* not commend them. He is further depicted as being *outside* this church, knocking to gain entrance!

Their plight is the ultimate result of not heeding the warnings given, starting with the church in Ephesus. Jesus had gone to them quickly, and had removed their candlestick. His love for them was not quenched, and thence this warning and call to a new generation.

Simply stated, it is this: "Do not follow the example of your fathers, but turn to Me and receive Me, and I will come in to your life and give you eternal and abundant life."

The modern Moslem city of Denizili, population 80,000, stands near the site of ancient Laodicea.

Neither Cold Nor Hot

Why would Jesus Christ write to the Laodicean church? Why would He write to a church that is dead? There are several explanations for this.

First, this church in Laodicea wasn't *always* dead. There is something that accrues continually from faith; the faith of the founding fathers was not totally lost.

Yes, the church in Laodicea missed it somewhere and disobeyed God in something in order to find itself in this sad, dead condition, but there were once those who had faith in this church — and God has made promises to those who have faith.

(We saw in scripture that God promised to bless down to a thousand generations those who love Him and keep His commandments.)

So Jesus is writing to this church to help it recover from its dead condition. As you look around at our present world, you'll see that He has already done this in many places; He's doing it currently; and He'll continue to do it on an even larger scale.

For example, a tremendous move of God is under way right now in the northern part of Europe; especially in denominational churches. When I was holding meetings there a few years ago, ministers and laypeople from denominations were being born again in every service.

There was such an anointing present, all we had to do was tell the people to open their mouth and God would fill it. They immediately began to speak in other tongues. But when we dealt with certain ministers to try to get them filled with the Holy Spirit, they couldn't receive. We found out the reason they couldn't was because they weren't saved! They had to go back and do the "first works" and get saved first!

As Jesus told the Laodiceans, "I would thou wert cold or hot. So then because thou art lukewarm, and neither cold nor hot, I will spue thee out of my mouth" (vv. 15,16).

Because you hold to your own ways and you won't acknowledge God's ways, Jesus said it would be better if you didn't acknowledge anything at all rather than be like that. Don't hold onto your own ways; let God have full control over your life.

Spiritual Poverty

"Because thou sayest, I am rich, and increased with goods and have need of nothing; and knowest not that thou art wretched, and miserable, and poor, and blind, and naked. . ." (v. 17). Wretched, miserable, poor, blind, and naked — that's the portrait of the spiritual condition of a person who is without God.

People who know God aren't blind in the spirit; they're not unclothed — they're the righteousness of God in Christ.

So this Laodicean church has come to the dead spiritual condition that Jesus warned the other churches about, and He's writing this letter to them to help them recover from that condition.

He tells them, "I counsel thee to buy of me gold tried in the fire, that thou mayest be rich; and white raiment, that thou mayest be clothed, and that the shame of thy nakedness do not appear; and anoint thine eyes with eyesalve, that thou mayest see" (v. 18).

All these benefits are the result of being born again and being filled with the Holy Spirit; these are the benefits we enjoy from the New Birth (or regeneration of the Holy Spirit) and the baptism in the Holy Spirit (or the fullness of the Holy Spirit).

Jesus: On the Outside Looking in

In verse 20, Jesus is not pictured as standing *within* this church; He's pictured *outside* it, isn't He? He said, "Behold, I stand at the door, and knock: if any man hear my voice, and open the door, I will come in to him, and will sup with him, and he with me."

He adds in verse 21, "To him that overcometh will I grant to sit with me in my throne, even as I also overcame, and am set down with my Father in his throne."

In contrast, the Book of Ephesians is written to a church that is *alive*. We read in Ephesians 2:1, "And you hath he quickened, who were dead in trespasses and sins. . . ." Verse 6: "And hath raised us up together, and made us sit together in heavenly places in Christ Jesus. . . ."

This is addressed to a church that is born again — a church that is alive — telling them they are seated with Jesus Christ in heavenly places.

In the letter to the Laodiceans, Jesus tells them that He grants this privilege of sitting with Him in His throne to *overcomers* (v. 21). The first step to overcoming is to enter into life from death. (There is a great deal more to overcoming than this first step, but this is where it begins.)

So in verse 20, we see Jesus standing at the door and knocking. He's not abandoning the Laodiceans; He's not casting them out; He's still dealing with them — but He's dealing with them from outside the church, not from within.

Trusting in Riches

We have seen that Laodicea was a very wealthy city in the natural. Furthermore, Laodicea and Hierapolis, which was a health spa, were across the river from Colossae. They held one thing in common: All these cities had become wealthy in this day. Laodicea had gone at least one step further and had become guilty of trusting in mammon.

You see, they trusted in their riches. They trusted in what they had in the natural. What eventually becomes of people like that? Trusting in natural things, they get separated from God, the evangelistic fire wanes, then flickers and dies. There is a picture of that right here in this letter to the Laodiceans.

"He that hath an ear, let him hear what the Spirit saith unto the churches" (v. 22).

All seven of the letters we have studied are meant to be applied to the whole Church Age. One letter is not to be applied to one part of the age, and another applied to an earlier or a later part of the age. Instead, the letters in their entirety represent an admonition to the entire Church, for this entire age.

If we are aware of what is happening in the church world today, we can see these same problems exist in every aspect Jesus has outlined them in to the seven ancient churches.

Also, the contents of these letters are not new admonitions from the Lord; you can find the same admonitions throughout the New Testament. They're all there.

Notice that Jesus counseled spiritually dead people to buy of Him gold tried in the fire (the Gospel truth) that they might be *truly* rich — *spiritually* rich.

Conclusion

We are instructed by the Word of God. We have been directed by that same Word. We are set free from bondage of every sort by God's Word.

We are the army of believers that God has and is still raising to finish the work of preaching to all the nations the Good News of Jesus Christ.

Jesus was the spiritual Rock (1 Corinthians 10:4) that followed Israel, His covenant people, in the wilderness. He followed them to bring them into the *land* that God had promised *them*. Their part was to pray, to believe His Word, and to keep their covenant with God.

But they wouldn't let Jesus take them into the land. God brought them out of Egypt — but He never got Egypt out of them! God's own people rebelled against Him, followed false gods, and walked in their own ways.

For too many years now, the modern Church has done something very much like that, so Jesus has not been able to bring us into all the glory and grace of the New Covenant. We have not been able to go into all the world as our dear Lord has commanded us.

We should recognize our sins and failures, admitting that *no one* but each of us is responsible for them. If we will overcome, as we have seen Jesus outline for us in these seven letters; if we will heed His warnings to His Body; if we will continue in those things He commends us for, we will be part of the victorious conclusion to this Age of Grace.

The time has come for you and me to go in and take our land for Jesus! He is our Victory; He is our Assurance; He is Lord of lords!

As Isaiah prophesied in Isaiah 60:1-5:

> **Arise, shine; for thy light is come, and the glory of the Lord is risen upon thee.**
>
> **For, behold, the darkness shall cover the earth, and gross darkness the people: *but the Lord shall arise upon thee,* and his glory shall be seen upon thee.**
>
> **And the Gentiles shall come to thy light, and kings to the brightness of thy rising.**
>
> **Lift up thine eyes round about and see: all they gather themselves together, they come to thee [as we "go ye" into all the world]....**
>
> **...the abundance of the sea shall be converted unto thee, the forces of the Gentiles shall come unto thee.**

A Prayer for the End Times

Let us pray this prayer together:

"O Lord, make me an instrument of your peace on earth, of spiritual warfare against every power, principality, or ruler of darkness in this world.

"Make me to be the MANIFESTED light of this world, and the salt of this earth, that You might receive glory, honor, praise, might, dominion, and power in the earth today.

"I receive it in Jesus' Name, and I thank You, Father, for providing my every need and making me more than a conqueror in this time. Amen."

Bibliography

The Revelation of John, Volume 1, William Barclay. Westminster Press, pp. 57-127.

The Seven Churches of Asia Minor, J. T. Marlin. Williams Printing Co.

The Illustrated Bible Dictionary, Volumes 1-3, Tyndale House Publishers.

Fox's Book of Martyrs, edited by William Byron Forbush. The John C. Winston Co.

Notes

Notes

To order books and tapes by Brian McCallum,
or to contact him for speaking engagements,
please write to:

Brian McCallum Ministries
12645 East 127th Street South
Broken Arrow, OK 74011